A **TRUE** BOOK™

Starting Your Own Business

NEL YOMTOV

Children's Press®
An Imprint of Scholastic Inc.
New York Toronto London Auckland Sydney
Mexico City New Delhi Hong Kong
Danbury, Connecticut

Content Consultant

Rodney Shrader, PhD

Professor, Denton Thorne Chair in Entrepreneurship

University of Illinois—Chicago

Chicago, Illinois

Library of Congress Cataloging-in-Publication Data

Yomtov, Nelson.

 Starting your own business / Nel Yomtov.

   pages cm.— (A true book)

 Includes bibliographical references and index.

 ISBN 978-0-531-24779-2 (lib. bdg.) — ISBN 978-0-531-28465-0 (pbk.)

1. New business enterprises—Juvenile literature. 2. Entrepreneurship—Juvenile literature. 3. Self-employed—Juvenile literature. I. Title.

 HD62.5.Y66 2013

 658.1'1—dc23   2013002374

All rights reserved. Published in 2014 by Children's Press, an imprint of Scholastic Inc. Printed in China 62

SCHOLASTIC, CHILDREN'S PRESS, A TRUE BOOK™, and associated logos are trademarks and/or registered trademarks of Scholastic Inc.

2 3 4 5 6 7 8 9 10 R 23 22 21 20 19 18 17 16 15

Front cover: Lemonade stand

Back cover: Bike shop owners

Find the Truth!

Everything you are about to read is true *except* for one of the sentences on this page.

Which one is **TRUE**?

T or F There are no disadvantages to owning your own business.

T or F A business plan explains your business in detail.

Find the answers in this book.

Contents

THE **BIG** TRUTH!

The Legal Forms of Business

When starting a new business, a person can learn a lot from other, similar businesses.

Charts and graphs can help you notice patterns in your business.

Motivated entrepreneurs across the country start new businesses every day.

CHAPTER 1

Be Your Own Boss!

Entrepreneurs are all around you. They own your local grocery store and bakery. They run hair salons and sell homemade items on the Internet. Have you ever dreamed about owning and operating your own business? If so, then you've already taken the first step toward becoming a successful entrepreneur. An entrepreneur starts and runs his or her own business, rather than working for someone else. Do you have what it takes to make your dream a reality?

About 500,000 new businesses are started in the United States each year.

The Pros and Cons

All entrepreneurs agree that there are many advantages *and* disadvantages to owning a business. One of the advantages is that business owners are independent. They can set their own working hours and do not have to follow someone else's orders. Owning a business can provide personal satisfaction by turning a hobby, interest, or special skill into moneymaking work. The financial reward from owning and growing a business can be far greater than from working for someone else.

About 67 percent of all millionaires in America own their own business.

It can be difficult for an entrepreneur to find time for a break, even to eat a meal.

The disadvantages of owning a business can be scary. You may work long hours, especially at first. You are not guaranteed a salary or benefits. At times, you may not even have enough money to pay yourself. Although you will work hard to succeed, your business may fail. If this happens, you may lose all the money you put into your business.

Even the smallest businesses require hard work and some creative thinking.

Your Personality Profile

Most entrepreneurs share certain personality traits. Here's a list of eight traits that most entrepreneurs share. Which ones do you have, and which ones need work?

1. Confidence
2. Willingness to take risks
3. Adaptability
4. Drive

5. Independence
6. Enthusiasm
7. Discipline
8. Competitiveness

Start With What You Know

Whether you decide to sell products or services, choose a business you know. It is best to work in a field with which you have some experience. Products are objects such as comic books, toys, T-shirts, video games, and food. Services are activities you sell to your customers, such as babysitting, tutoring, lawn mowing, and housecleaning. It's important to have a passion for the product or service you decide upon.

If you've ever helped take care of a baby brother or sister, you could use that experience to help start a babysitting business.

When there are already several established businesses of the same type in one area, it might be difficult to succeed with a competing business nearby.

CHAPTER 2

Checking Out the Competition

No matter which business you start, you're going to face competition. In business, competition consists of two or more businesses working to gain the most profits, sales, and customers. Before you take the plunge into entrepreneurship, you'll have to do your homework and learn as much as you can about your rivals. The information you uncover will help you better plan your business—and avoid making disastrous decisions that can ruin your dream.

Sizing Up Your Rivals

To gain an understanding of your competition's strengths and weaknesses, you must ask the right questions. What is your competitor doing right? Can you successfully copy these things? What can you improve? Can you make the product or service easier to find or buy? Are there "extras" you can offer that will pull customers to your business? To answer these questions, you've got to collect as much information as possible about each of your competitors.

For services such as repairing computers, think about how other computer repair businesses provide their services. Do employees visit customers at home? How do customers contact the business?

If you need ideas, try talking to friends and family members. What do they think about a product?

Suppose you want to bake and sell cookies. Check out your competition by visiting a local bakery. Which of its cookies look good? How are they priced? Ask the sales clerk what varieties sell best. Buy a few different cookies and do a taste test at home. How might you make tastier cookies? Take a look at the bakery's location. Are other bakeries nearby? Do you know a neighborhood that doesn't have a bakery but might need one?

Think about how your competitors describe their products in their advertisements. What factors do they mention or make sound important?

Check out the advertising that other companies similar to yours produce. Local newspapers, fliers, and mail-order catalogs might contain ads by other cookie sellers. Look them over carefully to learn what types of cookies your competitors sell and how much they charge for them. How could you offer a better range of cookies? Think about how you could advertise more effectively.

Don't be shy about talking to the owners of other businesses. Adult business owners might be happy to help you get started, even though you're the competition. Another way to get the scoop on your competition is to surf your competitors' Web sites. They might also have pages on Facebook or other social networking sites. You'll get to see what your rivals are doing locally, as well as around the world.

You might be surprised at how much advice other business owners are willing to give you.

Market Research

Another great way to prepare your business is learning more about your **market**. A market is the group of potential customers for your product or service. Market research is gathering information about the size and buying habits of your market. Sometimes entrepreneurs gather this information by interviewing potential customers. This is one way for you to learn if there is enough demand for your product or service to make your business succeed.

Even long-running, successful businesses continue to perform market research to improve the ways they present their products to customers.

Is Your Product Different?

One way to attract potential customers is to make your product or service different from those of your competitors. There may be differences in quality, price, or both. There can be differences in the way the product or service is advertised. There may also be differences in where and when the product or service is available. Do some market research with interviews or questionnaires to determine if those things that make your product different matter to your potential customers.

To make your business plan as helpful as possible, try to make it as detailed as you can.

Your Recipe for Success

So you've decided on the product or service you want to sell and have checked out the competition. Now it's time to start planning your business. This begins with writing an honest and carefully thought-out business plan. A business plan is your ideas and goals on paper. Basically, it's a way of reminding you and telling others where your company is going and where you want to take it.

Business plans usually map out a business's next three to five years.

Turning Talk Into Action

The goal of your business plan is to describe your business in detail. It can be only a few pages or more than 20 pages long. It details what your product or service is, how much money you plan to make, and how you'll reach your goals. Your plan should also discuss your competition, how you'll sell your product, and the other people involved in your business, if there are any.

Charts can help you condense a large amount of useful information into an easy-to-read visual aid for your business plan.

An investor lends money to a business, hoping to get more money back later.

One of the most important parts of your business plan discusses how much money you'll need to get your **start-up** off the ground and keep it running. You'll need to do some math to determine your start-up costs and how much you expect to earn over a given period of time. This information is important whether you ask people to **invest** in your business or not.

You can figure how much to charge customers for a service by deciding how much profit you want to make for each hour of work.

The goal of every entrepreneur is to make a profit on the goods or services he or she sells. A profit is the amount of money a business has earned, minus all the costs of running the business. You can try to estimate what your profits will be ahead of time. One way is to figure your start-up costs and then determine how much you'll earn over a period of time, such as a month.

Figure your earnings by multiplying how much you're going to charge by the number of customers you expect. Let's say you're going to clean houses and you think you'll have four clients who will each pay you $15 a week, for a total of $60 a week. In four weeks, or about one month, you'll earn 4 x $60, or $240. If your start-up costs total $140, your first month's profit would be $240 − $140, or $100.

The cost of sponges, mops, buckets, gloves, cleaners, and other supplies must be added up as part of the start-up costs for a cleaning business.

Funding Your Business

Perhaps you have enough money to meet your start-up costs and fund the business yourself. Before getting started, however, you might wonder what else you could do with your money. How could you spend it if you didn't start your business? This other way you could have used your money is called the **opportunity cost**. It is the profit that you *could* have made investing in something else.

Business in America Timeline

1873
Levi Strauss & Co. starts putting rivets, or metal pins, on their blue jeans.

1886
John Pemberton invents Coca-Cola.

1903
The Ford Motor Company is founded.

For your business, you may require investors, or people who help fund a business for a share of the profits. If so, your business plan must convince the investors that your business will succeed. Investors look at their investment in terms of opportunity cost. What investments are they passing up by investing in you? Investors also look at the "risk and reward" of your business. The bigger risk your business is, the greater **return** your investors expect.

1962

The first Walmart and Kmart stores open.

1975

Bill Gates and Paul Allen form Microsoft to develop software for personal computers.

2004

Facebook, the social networking Web site, is launched.

The Legal Forms of Business

The U.S. government expects you to pay taxes on the profits your business makes each year. To do this accurately, you must determine your business's legal structure. The three main types of businesses are sole proprietorships, partnerships, and corporations.

Sole Proprietorship

A sole proprietorship is a business owned and operated by one person. As sole proprietor, you make all the decisions, but you're also fully responsible for your company. If you are sued, you can lose all your savings, your house, and much more.

Partnership

A partnership has two or more co-owners of the business. In a *general* partnership, the partners share the decisions, the workload, and the legal responsibilities. In a *limited* partnership, general partners run the company. The limited partners are only investors. In a *limited liability* partnership, partners share the decisions and workload, but are less legally responsible for the business's debts.

Corporation

A corporation frees you from the financial and legal disadvantages of other forms of business. To incorporate, you must file papers with your state and pay a fee. If someone sues your corporation, he or she can only go after what the company owns, not your personal money or property.

FIFTH AVENUE

MEN'S SUITS

605 5TH AVENUE
THIRD FLOOR

40%-60%

OFF

Some businesses get
the word out about
their products by
hiring people to wear
advertisements and
hand out fliers.

Putting the Pieces Together

One way to help your business succeed is to tell people about it. You may offer the highest-quality product or service at the lowest price. But your business dream is sure to go up in smoke if you don't attract customers. You have to advertise. Then you need to close the deal with a potential customer: you have to make the sale.

More than $15 billion is spent on advertising to children in America each year.

Advertising Your Business

You see ads for products and services all the time on TV, in newspapers and fliers, and on the Internet and billboards. The simplest and least expensive type of advertising is a flier. You can leave them anywhere, or hand them out to people in your neighborhood. Keep your flier design simple. Use bold print and colors, and explain your product or service as simply as possible.

Your flier will need to compete with many others, so make sure it can catch people's attention and clearly explain your business.

The U.S. Postal Service offers special pricing for bulk mail such as direct mail advertising.

Direct mail advertising allows you to send fliers, letters, or brochures right to a potential customer's mailbox. When writing your mailing piece, come up with something that grabs your reader's attention. Perhaps it's a catchy phrase or a clever illustration showing the benefits of your service. You can buy mailing lists from special list companies. Mailing lists include the names and addresses of people to whom you can send your advertising.

Being polite and friendly encourages customers to use your business more than once.

Sell, Sell, Sell!

Once you've got a potential customer interested, it's time to make the sale. You might have to meet with that person or speak with him or her on the telephone. Either way, be pleasant. Most importantly, be honest. Find out what your customer wants. What's most important to the customer? Price? Quality? End your conversation by asking for your customer's order. And remember not to take "no" personally: most sales calls end with a rejection.

Supply and Demand

A market condition called supply and demand affects every business. Suppose you have many customers who want to hire you to care for their lawns. The demand for your service is high. This means you can charge more for your work. Soon, however, your friends start their own lawn-care businesses. The demand is now split among several businesses. With so many people supplying the same work, the prices for everyone's work— including yours—drop.

Staying on Top of Things

Keeping accurate and up-to-date records is an important part of every entrepreneur's business. Without them, you can't figure how much money you've earned, what your expenses are, or what your profit is. Records help you know what you've done, what you need to do, and most importantly, where your business is headed. Record keeping is part of what is called back-office operations. These activities support the main business of your company.

 Keep your records neatly organized in files or notebooks, or on a computer.

Invoicing

After providing your customer with a product or service, you'll need to give that person an **invoice**. An invoice is an itemized bill for what you've sold to your customer. Your invoice should be printed from a computer or neatly hand printed. It should include the date, your name, and your customer's name. It also needs a description of the work or item purchased and the total amount the customer owes. Keep a copy of all your invoices in an organized file.

Business owners often number their invoices to make it easier to keep track of them.

A book or computer file for keeping track of accounts is known as a ledger.

Where's the Money?

You may be asking, "How do I keep track of the money I'm owed and the money I owe to other people?" In a notebook or computer spreadsheet program, enter each financial activity that you perform. In one column, enter the amount of each invoice you've sent out. This amount that people owe you is called accounts receivable. In another column, enter each amount you owe others. This is your accounts payable.

Businesses big and small use profit-and-loss records to track their sales and expenses.

Keep another column of your income, or what people have already paid you. Another column will include your expenses, or what you have already paid others. Each month, subtract your total expenses from your total income. This will give you a profit-and-loss record of your business. After about three months, you'll know how your business is doing. With that information, you'll be able to make an effective **budget** to manage your business.

To make a budget, compare all of your income to all of your expenses. If you have more income than expenses, you're doing fine. If your expenses are greater, you have to cut them down or figure out how to increase your income. When you make your budget, you must also figure in your cash flow.

Just as you want your customers to pay you, you must always remember to pay the businesses to which you owe money.

Cash flow is all the money coming into and going out of your business. Sometimes you spend money and get paid at the same time. Sometimes this happens at different times. Your goal is to always have enough money to pay a bill when it comes in. Cash flow is not the same as your profit. Cash flow is how much money, if any, your business has at a given time.

With a little luck and a lot of hard work, your business will start to develop a following. Customers will line up for a chance to buy your product!

Even huge companies such as Apple started out as small businesses.

A Life-Changing Experience

Starting your own business takes lots of determination and commitment. It can be very rewarding or extremely disappointing. It can be thrilling one moment and scary the next. But if you like to be independent and aren't afraid to take risks, being an entrepreneur might be for you. Remember, every big company started small, so the sky's the limit for your business. Work hard— and keep your dream alive! ★

True Statistics

Number of small businesses in the United States: More than 27 million

Percent of all new jobs in the United States created by small businesses: Between 60 and 80 percent

Rate of success for small businesses in the United States: 31 percent survive the first 7 years

Number of small businesses with a Web site: About 49 percent

Percent of small businesses owned by the founder: 77 percent

Percent of small businesses run from the owner's home: 52 percent

Did you find the truth?

F There are no disadvantages to owning your own business.

T A business plan explains your business in detail.

Resources

Books

Bochner, Arthur, and Rose Bochner. *The New Totally Awesome Business Book for Kids*. New York: Newmarket Press, 2007.

Thompson, Gare. *What Is Supply and Demand?* New York: Crabtree Press, 2009.

Toren, Adam, and Matthew Toren. *Kidpreneur$: Young Entrepreneurs with Big Ideas!* Phoenix: Business Plus Media Group, 2009.

Visit this Scholastic Web site for more information on starting your own business:
★ www.factsfornow.scholastic.com
Enter the keywords **Starting Your Own Business**

Important Words

budget (BUHJ-it) — a plan for how much money you will earn and spend during a particular period of time

entrepreneurs (ahn-truh-pruh-NURZ) — people who start businesses and find new ways to make money

incorporate (in-KOR-puh-rate) — to make or become a corporation

invest (in-VEST) — to give or lend money to something, such as a company, with the intention of getting more money back later

invoice (IN-vois) — an itemized bill for goods sold to a customer or for work done or to be done for a customer

market (MAHR-kit) — a group of potential customers for your product or service

opportunity cost (ah-pur-TOO-ni-tee KAHST) — the profit a person could have made by not doing what he or she has chosen to do

return (ri-TURN) — money made as a profit

start-up (START-up) — a new company

Index

Page numbers in **bold** indicate illustrations

About the Author

Nel Yomtov is an award-winning author of nonfiction books for young readers. He has written several books for Scholastic, including titles in the Enchantment of the World series, the Cornerstones of Freedom series, and the Ancient World series. A native of New York City, Yomtov now lives in Long Island, New York, with his wife, Nancy. His son, Jesse, is a sportswriter.